Written by Heather Dakota
Photographs by Heather Dakota, Jacob Jansen,
Scott Zwiebel, and Daniel Jankowski
Designed by Bill Henderson and Daniel Jankowski

We'd like to thank Chris Soucy of Sixth Sense Savannah
Ghost Tour for his fabulous ghost stories.

Tangerine
press
an imprint of
SCHOLASTIC
www.scholastic.com

Copyright © 2008 Scholastic Inc.

Scholastic and Tangerine Press and associated
logos are trademarks of Scholastic Inc.

Published by Tangerine Press, an imprint of Scholastic Inc.,
557 Broadway; New York, NY 10012

10 9 8 7 6 5 4 3 2 1

Made in China

ISBN-10: 0-545-09932-3
ISBN-13: 978-0-545-09932-5

Scholastic Inc.
New York, NY

Scholastic New Zealand Ltd.
Greenmount, Auckland

Scholastic Canada Ltd.
Markham, Ontario

Scholastic Australia Pty. Ltd
Gosford NSW

Grolier International, Inc
Makati City, Philippines

This is a work of fiction. Most photographs are digitally enhanced. The
stories and photographs in no way authenticate the existence of ghosts.

Table of Contents

To all readers,

Beware! I have filled this book with things that make my skin crawl. It might do the same to you. You know, when the hairs on the back of your neck stand on end and goosebumps suddenly appear for no apparent reason. Strange!

I have been investigating paranormal activity for 15 years. I'm a ghost hunter. It's who I am. I'm skeptical by nature. I don't accept a ghost story as fact. I have to see the undisputed proof. And, I've seen my share.

I got caught up in the whole ghost hunting thing when I was a kid. Come on—what kid doesn't love a good ghost story? As I said, it started about 15 years ago when I was on a nighttime tour with my parents in St. Augustine, Florida. I'll tell you about that later. This was when I started keeping ghost journals. I have more than 100 of them filled with bizarre happenings and photos of things I can't explain. I have seen fakes and frauds, but there are some things that have scared the bejeebers out of me. These are the things that I'll try to explain in this book.

This is a culmination of all of my journals, the best stories and the best photos. I hope it doesn't scare you too much. Or maybe it should.

Sincerely,

Jack Bell

Jack Bell

P.S. Did you ever get the feeling that you're being watched or followed?

Ghosts: What Are They?

You've seen the movies and heard all the good stories. But what exactly is a ghost? The real answer is that no one really knows. There are thousands of theories. Here are a few:

I see dead people

Traditionally, people think of ghosts as the spirit of a person who has been stuck between this plane of existence and the next. A lot of times, a ghost will haunt the place where he or she died because it holds pleasant memories. These types of ghosts might even communicate with the living.

First impressions are everything

Some ghosts are "recordings" on a place where they once existed. A traumatic moment can leave an impression on a building or area. Then, it plays itself over and over again. Generally, it's a portion of the actual event. These types of ghosts usually don't interact with the living, but they can.

In my opinion, ghosts and hauntings are very real. I am a skeptic. I search out the cause of every phenomenon and debunk what I can. Still...there are some things I can't explain.

1 négatif seulement   1 ne

CADRAGE
CROPPING | V. | H. |

| 2½x3½ | 3½ x 5 | 4x5 | 5x5 | 5x7 | 8x8 | 8x10 |

I have a message for you

These ghosts are probably the most common. They appear to a loved one shortly after they have died. Usually, these spirits appear with the sole purpose of comforting the loved one or giving him or her a message. Sometimes, it's as simple as saying good-bye.

They're here!

People fear poltergeists the most. These entities can have the greatest effect on our world. This type of ghost is blamed for unexplained noises (such as wall-banging, footsteps, and music from nowhere), the TV or lights turning on and off, doors slamming, and even things being thrown across the room. Sometimes these spirits tug on clothes or hair, and the mean ones even have scratched and bitten people.

It's all in your head

I have to point out the fact that it could be just your imagination. Naysayers would like you to think that it's the living creating these phenomena. They say that we see ghosts because we want to see them. Since we know so little about the power of our own minds, it might be possible for us to produce ghosts.

How to Be a Ghost Hunter

Equipment needed:

Camera – A digital camera is a great way to check your photos right after your hunt.

Handheld tape recorder – One of the most important pieces of equipment. Use to interview witnesses or conduct Electronic Voice Phenomena (EVP) gathering.

Electromagnetic detector – Locates and tracks energy sources. The theory is that ghosts disrupt energy fields, so you'll get higher than normal readings if there is a paranormal entity around.

Pad of paper and pen or pencil – Log everything that happens. This is very important.

Compass – When the needle will not come to a precise heading, a spirit may be present.

Thermometer – A rapid drop of 10° or more could indicate a ghostly presence.

Watch or stopwatch – Log the time you start and stop and how long you were at a location.

Flour - If you see footsteps, it could be an actual person.

Thread - Use the thread to see if something moves.

Flashlight

Cell phone

Permission to investigate – Do not assume that you can ghost hunt anywhere you want. *Get permission every time!*

Candles are a great way to check for ghosts. Use the one from your kit to look for ghosts in your house. Does the candle stay on?

Interview Questions

Name of witness:_____

Address:_____

Phone number:_____

Occupants' names and ages:_____
_____

Occupants' religious beliefs:_____

How many people live here?_____
_____

How many pet(s)?_____
_____

How long occupied?_____

Age of site?_____

Any previous owners?_____

Do you know the history of the site?_____
_____

Any occupants with unexplained illnesses?_____
_____

Have there been any witnesses besides the occupants? _____
_____

Have there been any sightings? If so, when and where? _____
_____

Have there been any odors (perfumes, flowers, sulfur, ammonia)? If so, when and what?_____
_____

Have there been any sounds (footsteps, banging, knocks)? If so, when and where?_____
_____

Have there been any voices (whispering, yelling, crying, speaking, laughing)?
_____

Have any objects moved? If so, when and where?_____
_____

Ghosts: Caught on Film

You can take a photo of a ghost. They can look like orbs, mists, or something like a tornado.

You'll need:
Digital or film camera
(If using a film camera, use at least 400 speed 35 mm film.)

☠ Take note of where lights are located. When you develop your film, you'll know that it's a real-world light and not an orb.

☠ Dust, dirt, and bugs will look like orbs.

☠ Don't bother looking through the viewfinder. Hold the camera out at arm's length and aim at any area of your choice.

☠ Make notes about streetlights, reflective surfaces, and polished tombstones.

☠ If you're working with others, let each other know when you are taking a picture so you don't get a double flash.

☠ If it's cold, make sure your breath doesn't get in front of the camera. It'll look like ectoplasm.

☠ Take photos everywhere. If you think you see something, take a picture.

☠ If you catch something in your flash, keep shooting. You may be near a ghost.

Note: Ghosts tend to disrupt electronic equipment. If your tape recorder, camera, or video recorder doesn't work, there might be spirit activity in the area.

How to Hear the Voice of a Ghost

Electronic Voice Phenomena, or EVP, is the recording of a spirit's voice. When this phenomenon was first discovered, there were many skeptics. It's very difficult to get an EVP, so be patient and persistent!

You'll need:

A tape recorder

- Set the tape recorder in one place. Just let it run as you walk around.

- Introduce the recording session and everyone who is present.

- Ask questions of the spirits.

One of the first recordings was of a haunted farmhouse. It was haunted by the spirit of a little girl. Her voice was clearly heard on the tape recorder calling for her mother.

Examples:

- *Welcome all spirits in the area.*

- *How did you die?*

- *Why are you here?*

- Make sure you listen to the entire tape with earphones. EVPs may not have been heard while you were recording, but they might be heard when you review the tape.

- Make notes of any unusual sounds or those of your fellow ghost hunters.

Signs of a Haunting

True hauntings are very rare, but there may be indications that something strange is going on around you.

- ☠ You may hear unexplained noises (footsteps, knocks, banging, scratching sounds). These noises can be soft or loud.

- ☠ Sometimes a door will open or close by itself. If this happens, check for breezes that might explain this. Rarely will you witness the door opening or closing. You could find that furniture has moved, too.

- ☠ Lights may turn on and off. Like the door, it is rare that you will actually see this happen. This can happen to TVs, radios, and other electronic equipment.

- ☠ Items disappearing and reappearing is a common phenomenon with a true haunting. This phenomenon is when you cannot find a regular item, like your house key. You look high and low, but it's definitely gone. Then, it appears exactly where you normally keep it. This could take days or weeks.

- ☠ In a haunting, you can see unexplained shadows. These are usually things that you see out of the corner of your eye. Sometimes the shadow has a vague human form.

- ☠ Occasionally, a family pet will begin to act strange. These strange animal behaviors can be an indication of a haunting. Dogs can bark at the unseen, cower without reason, or refuse to enter a room. Cats may seem to "watch" something cross the room, or arch their back and hiss at nothing. Animals have stronger senses than humans. Watch them carefully.

- It is not uncommon to feel as though you're being watched. But in combination with some of the other phenomena, and if it's consistent, it could mean something.

- Being watched is one thing, but actually being touched is something completely different. You could feel something brush past you, touch your hair, a hand on your shoulder or a push, a poke, or a nudge.

- Voices or unexplained music are great indications of a haunting. Cries, whispers, muffled voices, or your name being called are all credible phenomena. If another person hears something, too, it is even more credible.

- Classic signs of a haunting are hot and cold spots. Use your thermometer to find out if there are hot or cold spots around you. It could mean you're close to a spirit.

- Unexplained smells can accompany other phenomena, like shadows, voices, or touches. The smell can be the fragrance of perfume, cooking, or even a foul odor.

- Witnessing objects hovering or moving is extremely rare, but is an extreme indication of a haunting.

- If you see unexplained writings on paper or a wall, then you could be in the middle of a poltergeist phenomenon.

- Actually seeing a spirit or apparition is also very rare, but human-shaped mists or shapes are definite indications of a haunting.

My loving Pug puppy, Taz, barked at the ceiling often. There were no strange noises, strange lights, or any real-world reasons for my poor pup to be acting so strangely, except for the unexplained shadows that I used to see out of the corner of my eye.

St. Augustine

I got started in ghost hunting when I was 13. I was on vacation with my parents in St. Augustine, soaking up the Florida Sun. We were on a nighttime tour of the city, passing a cemetery on Cordova Road. It was 9:17 P.M. I remember this because I had just looked at my watch. When I looked up, there was a little boy about four years old in a huge oak tree looking down and giggling. I nudged my mother and made a snide comment about a young boy out so late by himself. My mother looked at me like I was out of my mind, and said, "Jack, what are you talking about?" She didn't see anything, so I asked the tour guide, who proceeded to tell me about a young boy who died of yellow fever in the 1820s. He has been hanging out in that tree ever since. The tour guide laughed and said, "Boy, you've just seen a ghost."

Staff at Hull House in Chicago are reporting footsteps, voices, cold touches, and bumps by the unseen.

Call Casablanca Inn. The innkeeper is making an appearance with her lantern again.

Gambler ghost making appearance again at the St. James Hotel in Cimarron, New Mexico... Book room 18 on April 20.

13

The Wanderers, Massachusetts, US.

In 1770, Peter Rugg and his daughter Jenny were on their way home to Boston after doing some business in Concord. On their way home, a wicked storm came up. Peter and Jenny never made it home to Boston.

In the 1820s, a stagecoach driver said he had seen the rickety old carriage hundreds of times. A storm always follows.

The Myrtles, St. Francisville, Louisiana, US.

This plantation, located between New Orleans and Natchez, is now an inn. The primary spirit is Chloe, a slave who had worked in the main house. After many warnings about her habit of eavesdropping, Chloe listened at the door one time too many. Mr. Woodruffe, owner of the plantation, had her left ear cut off as punishment. She has haunted the place since her death.

Received a story about a house in Hemingway, South Carolina. The clie[nt] says that something grabbed her hair and that she couldn't breathe i[n] the living room. Must call client back. Research shows that a little boy, 5-8 years old, drowned in the pool. Advis[e] not to purchase.

Dear Mr. Bell,

I heard about you through one of your newspaper articles. I'm writing to tell you about the deserted mental hospital in Newtown, Connecticut, very close to where I used to live. It opened in 1933 and closed down in 1995. The staff lived in absolutely beautiful buildings, but other buildings give me an overwhelming heaviness. There are darkly lit tunnels under the entire complex, too.

I've always been warned not to go there. However, friends of mine have seen "things." In 1978, one friend had a kid walk up to her and ask where to find his mother. He said his name was John. My friend turned around to look for an adult. When she turned back around, John was gone. Come to find out, John passed away at that institution in the early 1940s.

Perhaps you can get to the bottom of some of the phenomena that have happened over the years.

Sincerely,

Mary

Mary

15

The Hitchhiker, British Columbia, Canada

A young woman from the University of British Columbia met a most untimely end when she died in a high-speed crash. She waits on University Boulevard for a ride home, but when a car stops, she vanishes.

Request permission to do an investigation at the Vogue Theatre in Vancouver.

Firkins' House owners report the presence of a very friendly young man, who is also a ghost.

Dear Jack,

We met on your trip to Toronto, Canada, last spring. You said you would take a look at my photo and let me know what you thought. I've included the photograph, and here is the story behind it.

When I was a young girl in Ottawa I lived down the street from the Brown family. On my way to my grandmother's house, I would pass by the Brown house. It had one of the most beautiful yards in the area. In the front of the house was a large bay window. An old woman would sometimes stand in that window as I walked by. She was always dressed in black with something white in her hand. I saw her about three times.

The last time I was in town, I went by the house. The old woman was in the window again, so I took this photo. What do you think?

Sincerely,

Leslie

Leslie

Woman in Canada
reports her bed
s haunted.

Azeman, Surinam, South America

The Azeman is a ghostly woman who haunts the villages of Surinam in northeastern South America. The ghost bites a piece of flesh from the big toe of a sleeping person. Don't fall asleep!

Bakas, a secret society in Haiti, reportedly are returning from the grave. Get permission from government to investigate.

The Bus, Panama, Central America

A bus traveling near Panama City reported the sudden appearance of an extremely ill American soldier. He was lying across the backseat of the bus. The pale man asked to be dropped off at a clinic, but then suddenly disappeared.

NAME

19

Investigation:
Savannah, Georgia, U.S.

Address: 432 Abercorn St.; Savannah, Georgia (Historic District, Calhoun Square) Note: House is vacant.

House History: House possibly built over the graves of slaves who died during the yellow fever epidemic of 1850. 1860s – Retired colonel chains his daughter to a chair and leaves her in the front window. The young girl dies of dehydration. 1880s – Three young girls murdered in first floor parlor. The newspapers attribute the murders to the "Savannah Ripper." 1970s – House was used by an evil cult. Sacrifices rumored to have taken place on second floor. 1990s – House rented to 12 college students. They add a 13th student to help with expenses. Student lived in the upstairs sunroom. Student disappeared and was never heard from again.

Reports: Owners and renters have reported whispers, dog footsteps, little girl laughing, shadows, and hot and cold spots. Owner refuses to let anyone live in the house.

Feelings: Overwhelming fear and sense of being watched, especially from upstairs windows.

Investigation: Set up voice recorders and video cameras throughout the house. Carried camera, electromagnetic detector, and temperature gauge. No bugs present and very little light from the park, traffic was minimal. Investigation took place from 9:30 P.M. to 5:00 A.M.

Outcome: EVP downstairs registers a lot of static, mumbling voices and possibly giggling. EVP upstairs heard the words, "Get out." Photos outside the house show orbs, shadowy faces, and glowing eyes. Video equipment and camera inside did not work. Temperatures fluctuated 20 to 30 degrees throughout the house and within the same room. There were definite hot and cold spots, especially in the living room.

Conclusion: Definitely haunted. I'm not going back!

Lights are on, but
no one lives here!

21

Spinetingler: Canada, Ghost Train

In the early 1900s, a railway fireman and a CPR line engineer, Twohey, were a few miles outside of Medicine Hat when a light appeared on the tracks in front of them. It looked like another train. Twohey yelled for them to jump off but the train was too close. Then, the train veered off and went past them. Its whistle was blowing and they could see the passengers staring at them. There was only one track and the wheels of the train were not touching the ground! A few weeks later, engineer Nicholson and the same fireman were on another night run when the same train light came toward them. As before, the train raced passed them. The fireman decided that was that. He requested a transfer to work in the train yard. In early July, a report came in that there had been an accident. Two trains collided just outside of Medicine Hat, on the exact spot of the reported ghost train. Seven people were killed, including two engineers, Twohey and Nicholson.

Investigation:
South America, Machu Picchu

Where: Peru

History: The pre-Columbian city created by the Incas is located on a mountain ridge in the Urubamba Valley in Peru. It was forgotten for centuries, but was rediscovered in 1911 by archaeologist Hiram Bingham. It is surrounded by jungle.

Reports: Paranormal and enlightening experiences.

Feelings: Overwhelming joy.

Investigation: Received permission from the Peruvian government to spend the night with a government representative (so we don't harm the site). The peak is 7,980 ft. (2,430 m) above the forest floor. We are only allowed to set up voice recorders. Each of us will carry a handheld digital camera, thermometer, and electromagnetic detector. Investigation started at 10 P.M., ended 5 A.M.

Outcome: Whispers caught on the EVP, nothing distinguishable. Nothing appears in any of the photos.

Conclusion: A very ancient site for sure, but we did not gather enough evidence to say it is definitely haunted.

In 2006, my daughter saw a young girl in our apartment who was about 10 or 11 years old. I saw something, too, out of the corner of my eye, like a burst or something in motion. When we moved out, I didn't think much more about it, until I started working with a woman who, come to find out, used to live in that same apartment. In 2000, her daughter told her about feeling a presence.

23

Travels in Europe

Whitechapel, East End, London, England

The Whitechapel area of East London was built on the remains of an old Roman settlement. In the Dark and Middle Ages, the area was the hub of business. However, during Elizabethan times, it was the place of notorious soldiers, bars, and fights. The people in this area lived in extreme poverty. It was also the scene of the most brutal murders ever recorded—those of Jack the Ripper. The victims are said to haunt the East End. You could possibly see the ghosts of Roman soldiers, a murderous sea captain, and a scary black carriage drawn by white glowing horses that disappears as quickly as it appears.

Make reservations in Edinburgh, Scotland. Much to investigate.

TIMES

Price twenty pence

WEDNESDAY AUGUST 5 1981

Spirits acting up again in Derbyshire

By Our Staff

Ghosts are no longer waiting until the Sun goes down. They are coming out during the day. The Bell Inn report that the young servant girl is making appearances in daylight. She was murdered in 1745 by the Jacobite army.

VERDE & CO

Contact Donald Rumbelow regarding any information about ghosts of Whitechapel, possibly in connection with Jack the Ripper murders.

Edinburgh, Scotland

There are dozens of strange occurrences and unexplained photos both inside and outside the most haunted house in Scotland. It was built in the 1600s to hold hundreds of people during the 1645 plague. Some of the ghosts to encounter are a ghostly piper, a headless drummer, spirits of French and colonial prisoners, and even a dog that haunts the cemetery. In 2001, a group of 240 volunteer ghost hunters walked through the castle with tons of ghost-busting equipment. The volunteers had no knowledge of any previous reports. The group reported drops in temperature, shadowy figures, burning sensations, being touched, and clothing being tugged on.

Call Dolphin Inn on Queen Street. The staff reports that the gas taps are being turned off again.

25

Mary Kings Close should be investigated! It is the spot where victims of the Black Death plague were sealed up to die.

Book tickets to Edinburgh

Stonehenge is a prehistoric monument in the English countryside about 8 mi. (12.87 km) north of Salisbury. Archaeologists believe the stones were put up around 2200 B.C. No one really knows what Stonehenge was originally intended for, but it has been the site of Druid celebrations for centuries. There have been many paranormal reports.

NAME

No.

27

Stockholm, Sweden

There are several instances of hauntings that need to be investigated. Look into the Royal Palace. It is reported to be haunted by the White Lady and the Gray Man. The White Lady appears when someone in the royal family is about to die. The Gray Man is said to be the ghost of Birger Jarl, the founder of Stockholm.

The Stockholm Metro is supposedly haunted by a ghost train, *Silverpilen*.

Dear Signor Bell,
Please come to see the Coliseum. We are having more and more ghost activity in recent weeks. Perhaps you can tell us why the increase.

I look forward to hearing from you.

Kind regards,

Giuseppe Casalese
Security Guard, Roman Coliseum

Get airline tickets to Stockholm for investigation

Babenhausen Kaserne Museum, Germany

Reports tell about a woman who keeps
calling the museum but talks backward.
The lights turn on and off by themselves.

Coliseum, Rome, Italy

The Roman Coliseum held events for the
citizens of Rome. Gladiator fights, lions
feeding on prisoners of war, and even mock
sea battles took place in the Coliseum.
Tour guides and visitors have reported
cold spots, being touched or pushed,
whispers, the sound of swords clanking,
and the sounds of wild animal noises.

The servants
at Versailles in
France have
been seeing
ghosts with no
heads. No doubt
from all the
beheadings!

Auschwitz Concentration Camp, Oswiecim, Poland

Auschwitz concentration camp was in operation from May 1940 to January 1945. Estimates show that 2.1 to 2.5 million people were killed in the gas chambers during that time—approximately 2 million were Jewish. There is an overwhelming sense of melancholy and foreboding as you enter these camps. Visitors have broken down in tears for no reason, and some never complete the tours. It has been reported that even the birds do not sing in the trees around the death camp. The environment is also withering. The silence is almost deafening. There have been reports of cold spots and intense emotions. Many recent tour groups have reported hearing voices and being touched and grabbed. Hear the words "Please" and "Leave." Photographs over the years have shown misty spirits, shadows, lights, and orbs. No investigation group has revealed their findings. Given its past, this could be the most haunted place on Earth.

Contact Auschwitz for permissions.
Can we investigate at night?

Heard word today about a water goblin under the Charles Bridge in Prague. It is said to eat those who jump off the bridge.

Check out
Raynham Hall
when in England.
It has best ever
ghost photo.

Investigation:
UK, Tower of London, England

History: The history of the Tower is extensive. On the bank of the River Thames, the Tower of London has held prisoners like Queen Ann Boleyn, Guy Fawkes, and even Queen Elizabeth I.

Reports: Ghosts have been sighted throughout the complex. There have been reports of whispers, cries, touches, and spooky sounds.

Feelings: During the day, there was a feeling of history, but nothing menacing. Profound sadness felt in the sanctuary.

Investigation: We must be with a Beefeater at all times. No cameras are allowed in the church. We will have cameras outside and trained on the block where many lost their heads. There are videos in many of the rooms within the tower. Audio recordings are allowed in the church. We will be carrying cameras, thermometers, and electromagnetic devices. Investigation began at 9 P.M., ends 6 A.M.

Outcome: Video camera in several of the rooms captured shadowy figures, but nothing definite. Cameras didn't reveal anything. Audio recordings captured whispers, but nothing decipherable.

Conclusion: Will have to continue investigation. There is definitely something here, but it would take a lot of time to gather all the information needed.

Europe, Paris Catacombs, France

Address: Paris, France

History: City planners in Paris decided to move the dead. Millions of dead Parisians were quietly deposited along the walls of the dark passageways that lie beneath the city.

Reports: Many visitors to the world beneath the streets have reported seeing ghostly figures. Some tours have been cut short because ghosts follow the living during tours. Photos have shown ghostly orbs, mists. And EVPs have been recorded throughout the passageways. There are many reports of people who have gone into the catacombs alone, but who have never returned.

Feelings: A lot of unease.

Investigation: Audio and video recorders will be set up every 10 ft. (3 m). All of us will carry digital cameras, infrared lights, night vision binoculars, and electromagnetic devices. Investigation started at 9 P.M., ended 6 A.M.

Outcome: Whoa! We have multiple EVPs, some are just whispers, but some are definitely human voices. Video recorders and cameras picked up orbs and shadows. Several of us were touched—one had hair brushed from face. Electromagnetic readings were off the charts.

Conclusion: There is definitely paranormal activity in those passageways.

Transylvania is
another stop.
Several newspapers
requesting Dracula
investigation.

35

Travels in Africa

Spinetingler: The Visitor

A friend had been visiting me. He left my flat at 2 A.M. As I turned around to close the door, someone whispered my name in my right ear. I thought it was my friend, but he was already a floor below. I figured it was a combination of being tired and an overactive imagination. As I stepped farther into the room, a feeling of terror came over me. As I looked into the living room, a dark figure was sitting on the couch. Its head turned toward me and it stood up. The figure was so tall its head touched the ceiling. I ran for my bedroom and slammed the door. There were two taps on my door and then a loud bang. Then, all was quiet.

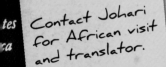

Contact Johari for African visit and translator.

After a trip through the Cape of Good Hope Nature Reserve, we were driving along Chapman's Peak Road. We came across a procession of monks walking down the road. We thought this very strange. When we stopped at our hotel and told our tale of the monks, we were told that these monks do not exist. This could be something for you to look into.

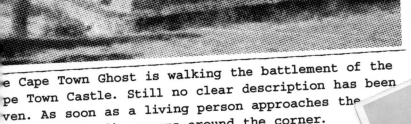

e Cape Town Ghost is walking the battlement of the
pe Town Castle. Still no clear description has been
ven. As soon as a living person approaches the
parition, it disappears around the corner.

37

An American team of archaeologists has been spending time in the Valley of the Kings. They have been hearing whispers and seeing ghostly figures. Get permission from the Supreme Council of Antiquities in Cairo to join the team in Egypt.

Africa, Goede Hoop, South Africa

Where: South Africa

History: The castle was built in 1666. It took eight years to complete the building. During high tide, the moat fills with water. There is a windowless dungeon with cells full of graffiti. During winter floods, the water rose 3 ft. (0.9 m). Many of the convicts in the cells drowned.

Reports: In 1915, a short, shadowy figure was seen on the battlement. This ghost has been seen many times over the years. Footsteps have been heard in the same area of the castle. A black hound jumps at visitors, only to disappear at the last minute. Laughing and arguing have been heard throughout the castle, especially around the guard room. Lady Anne Barnard is one of the favorite castle ghosts. She was the governor's wife.

Feelings: Definite feeling of paranormal activity. Feeling like we're being watched.

Investigation: Video cameras and audio equipment set in rooms where paranormal activity has been said to take place. Digital cameras will be handheld. Thermometers and electromagnetic device brought with us. Investigation started at 7 P.M., ended 5 A.M.

Outcome: Wow! This was an incredible investigation. Video camera shows figures moving through rooms and hallways. Several photos were taken, but did not show up the next day. EVPs all over the tapes. Will need to comb through carefully.

Conclusion: Definitely haunted!

Travels in Australasia

Rookwood Cemetery, Sydney, Australia

Rookwood Cemetery is the final resting place of approximately one million people. People have reported orbs, flashing lights, eerie mists, and ghostly figures walking or floating through the cemetery.

While in Taiwan, visit Xinhai Tunnel. Old woman ghost said to be cleaning the road.

Officer Steven _____ stopped a 1953 black Chevy that was doing circles. After stopping the vehicle and asking the driver to step out of the car, the officer put his hand on his pistol. The driver and a passenger stepped out of the car and moved toward the officer. They stopped about 5 ft. (1.5 m) from the officer and their heads spun around 180 degrees.

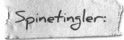

Spinetingler:

Rajasthan Alwar, Bhangarh Ruins

The Bhangarh Ruins in India are known for causing fear. Most people hear strange sounds of music and dancing at night when there's no one around. The city was established in 1631, but it was abandoned in a hurry due to a curse put on the town. Rumor has it that anyone who stays there after dark has never returned. People who have visited say there is a feeling of anxiety and restlessness.

A 10-year haunting is solved in the GuangXi province in China. Owners of the apartments in the five-story building tell of spooky sounds coming from somewhere in the house. Turns out there were 10 catfish in the pipes of the building. Now, that's fishy!

Fly to Singapore?
Supposed to be
most haunted
place on Earth.

Australia, Palmyra Island Atoll

History: Palmyra is an uninhabited island near the center of the Pacific Ocean. It is 1,000 mi. (1,609.3 km) southwest of Hawaii. Rain forest jungles rule the interior of the island, and coral reefs surround the island.

Reports: Can an entire island be haunted? Sailors say that the island is full of trouble. World War II veterans report that aggressive sharks took several victims every month. Even fish that swim in the waters are poisonous. Legends tell of the island appearing out of nowhere and disappearing just as quickly. There are also tales of pirate gold.

Feelings: Yikes! It's not often that I don't want to go near a place, but this is one of them. It could be the poisonous fish and dangerous reef sharks.

Investigation: Will investigate from the boat. Investigation started 5 P.M., ended 3 A.M.

Outcome: Well, not so exciting. A feeling of danger is all we got from this one.

Conclusion: Need to get on the island to investigate further.

Ghost Ships

Ghost ships can be explained as an apparition over water (usually a sailing ship) or ships floating around without a crew. A ghost ship also can be a real-world ship crewed by ghosts. Ghost ships usually appear on a stormy night.

Kaz II

A catamaran named *KAZ II* was discovered without its crew near the Great Barrier Reef off the coast of Queensland, Australia, in April 2007. When the ship was boarded, the engine was running, a laptop computer was on, the radio and GPS were working, and a meal was ready to be eaten, but the three-man crew was not on board. All the sails were up, but one was shredded. The life jackets, survival equipment, and emergency beacon were all on the yacht. The crew never was found.

The Flying Dutchman

The *Flying Dutchman*, one of the most famous ghost vessels, set sail in 1751. Legend has it that the ship was seeking shelter in the Cape of Good Hope, but as punishment for his blasphemy, Captain Hendrik van der Decken must sail until doomsday. The appearance of this vessel signals doom and tragedy for the sailors who see it. The *Flying Dutchman* brings dangerously bad weather and has been spotted many times in the last two centuries. King George V of England writes:

"At 4 a.m. the Flying Dutchman crossed our bows. A strange phantom ship all aglow... The officer of the watch from the bridge clearly saw her, as did the quarterdeck midshipman, who was sent forward at once to the forecastle; but on arriving there was no vestige nor any sign whatever of any material ship. Thirteen persons altogether saw her at 10:45 A.M."

Mary Celeste

On November 5, 1872, a great sailing ship, the *Mary Celeste,* set sail from New York Harbor bound for Genoa, Italy, with a crew of eight, the captain, and the captain's wife and daughter. On December 4, the *Mary Celeste* was spotted by the *Dei Gratia* between the Azores and the coast of Spain. The captain of the *Dei Gratia* reported the sails of the *Mary Celeste* were flapping, but there was plenty of food and fresh water, the crew's belongings hadn't been touched, and its cargo of 1,700 barrels was still on board. However, the eight crew members, Captain Briggs, his wife, and his daughter were not aboard and never were found.

Dutch Freighter Ourang Medan

In 1948, many ships responded to a Morse code message from the Dutch freighter *Ourang Medan.* The ship was found off the coast of Indonesia. The boarding party found the crew frozen, teeth bared, and looking at the Sun. Before they could tow the ship back to port, it exploded and sank. The deaths never have been explained.

No reflection of the boat in the water?

HMS Eurydice

During a blizzard in 1878, a 26-gun frigate capsized and sank in Sandown Bay near England. The phantom vessel, *HMS Eurydice*, has been spotted by sailors over the years. In 1998, Prince Edward of England and a film crew saw the three-masted ship off the Isle of Wight. They even captured the ghost ship on film.

Lady Lovibond

The *Lady Lovibond* was wrecked in the area of Goodwin Sands in the British Isles. The ship is seen every 50 years.

Queen Mary

The ocean liner *RMS Queen Mary* sailed the North Atlantic Ocean from 1936 to 1967. It was built in Scotland. During World War II, the ship transported troops. The *Queen Mary* is permanently berthed in Long Beach, California, where it serves as a museum. There are numerous ghosts that haunt the rooms and hallways of the legendary vessel.

So, do you believe in ghosts yet?